MW01462586

Mali: Today and Long Ago

9/22/07

To Mrs. Ouelle
Reading is thinking! Enjoy
thinking + learning in
this book —

by

Melanie Zucker Stanley

Melanie Zucker Stanley

FOXHOUND PUBLISHING, LLC
Glen Allen, Virginia

Thanks to the following for their scholarly expertise and help: Veronika Jenke, curator of education, National Museum of African Art; Edward De Carbo,Ph.D., former director of education at the National Museum of African Art; John Franklin, program manager and curator of the Mali Program Center for Folklife and Cultural Heritage at the Smithsonian Institution; and especially to Robin-Edward Poulton (Macky Tall), Ph.D., a man who lived in Mali and loves the people there.

I would also like to thank the following educators for reading and commenting on my manucript: Kevin Simpson, Michele Scadron, Jean Frey, Sara Shoob, Beth English. I especially thank my husband, Tim Stanley, for his support and literary suggestions.

Foxhound Publishing, LLC
P.O. Box 5543
Glen Allen, Virginia
www.foxhoundpublishing.com

Produced by Shoreline Publishing Group LLC
Santa Barbara, California
Designer: Rave & Associates

Library of Congress CIP data available.
ISBN: 1-58796-009-5

Printed in the United States of America.

Contents

Mali

THE CONTINENT OF AFRICA has more than 50 countries. One of these countries is Mali [MAH-lee].

Mali is in West Africa. The huge Sahara [suh-HARE-uh] Desert, the biggest desert in the world, is to the north. The Sahara Desert runs through some of Mali's land in the north. Most of the people of Mali live in the land south of the desert.

Mali is in an area known as West Africa. Some people think that Mali is shaped like a butterfly.

These girls in Mali are dressed for a festival.

THE PEOPLE

Almost 11 million people live in Mali today. Like America, many different groups of people live there. The Bambara [bahm-BAHR-ah], Fulani [foo-LAH-nee], and Malinke [muh-LINK-uh] are some of the different people who live in Mali.

Many people of Mali are farmers. They grow food such as rice and millet (a kind of grain). Some people are ***herders***. They raise animals for food and milk. They move their animals from place to place. Fishermen live by the river and sell what they catch. Traders sell their goods. Most of the people are farmers, herders, fishermen, and traders. But some people work as doctors, teachers, artists, or in other jobs.

Water IS LIFE

MALI IS A VERY HOT, dry country with very little rainfall. Water is everything to the people of Mali. When it does not rain, crops do not grow. Then the people and animals do not have food.

The Niger [NYE-jer] River is important to Mali. People use it for drinking and watering their crops and animals. River boats carry goods, animals, and people to towns and markets.

Mali today is one of the poorest countries in the world. A long time ago, Mali was different!

The Niger River in Mali is important for both people and animals.

MALI'S GREAT PAST

Mali's people are proud of their history. They tell stories about Mali long ago. Mali started as a small ***kingdom*** long before Christopher Columbus came to the Americas. After many years, Mali grew to become a large empire.

The Empire of Mali was one of the richest empires in the world!

West Africa
LONG AGO

THERE WAS ANOTHER KINGDOM in West Africa that grew to be rich and strong before Mali. That kingdom was called Ghana [GAHN-ah], and it started almost 2,000 years ago. Trading gold made Ghana rich. Ghana was so rich it was called the "Land of Gold." After many years, Ghana began to have problems and other people took over that kingdom. This next great kingdom was Mali.

These gold earrings were made by the Fulani people sometime in the 20th century.

This is a chi wara, a mythical and ancient creature who helped the Bambara people learn to farm. This figure was worn on the head of dancers like a hat during celebrations.

How History Tells Its Story

How do we know the stories of Mali's history?

- Arab traders went to Mali and wrote about what they saw there.
- ***Griots*** (storytellers) in West Africa pass down the stories of Mali's history.
- ***Archaeologists*** study manmade things from the past called artifacts. From artifacts, archaeologists learn about people who lived a long time ago. They work with historians to put the stories together, like pieces of a puzzle.

BEGINNINGS

MALI BEGAN AS A SMALL ***kingdom*** in West Africa. The people who lived there were called the Malinke. The Malinke people lived in groups called ***clans.*** Each clan had a king, but the clans did not always get along and often fought. So the kings met to make a plan. To stop the fighting, they decided to choose one king to be the leader. Malinke kings ruled Mali for many years.

Some Malinke people in Mali still live in traditional huts like this one.

Hunters in Sundiata's time might have worn a shirt like this. It is made of an animal skin. The shirt is decorated with an animal horn and strips of fabric

The Real Lion King

One king was different from the others. He turned the small kingdom of Mali into a large and powerful empire. This king's name was Sundiata Keita [Soon-JAH-tah KAY-tah]. Keita means "lion" in the Malinke language. Some people called Sundiata the Lion of Mali. Sundiata was a hunter who was strong and smart like a lion.

Speaking of Mali

Many Malinke people still live in Mali today. The Malinke are part of a language group in West Africa called the Mande [MAHN-day]. Mande is not just one language such as Spanish or English. Mande is the name for a group of languages spoken in West Africa.

Sundiata:
A GREAT KING

WEST AFRICAN GRIOTS TELL the story of Sundiata. It is said that he was born about 800 years ago, but no one knows the exact year. His father, King Fatta, was told, "Your son will be the greatest king Mali has ever had." But something went wrong. As a boy, Sundiata was not able to walk or speak. No one knew why. His mother tried many things to help her son. Nothing worked, and so Sundiata's half-brother became king. This made Sundiata's mother sad.

Sundiata worked hard and learned to speak and walk. Some griots say that a village blacksmith made iron braces for his legs.

Sundiata's mother took him far away from Mali to live. She wanted Sundiata to grow up safely. Some day he would return to Mali and be king.

No one knows what Sundiata looked like. He may have looked and dressed like this.

Sundiata grew to be strong and smart. He learned to be a great hunter, to ride a horse, and to use a bow and arrow in battle. Finally, Sundiata became the king of Mali in about 1230. However, a king named Sumanguru [soo-mahn-GOO-roo] wanted power in Mali.

Sundiata
SHOWS THE WAY

SUNDIATA'S FIRST JOB WAS TO get rid of Sumanguru. The two kings met in battle. Sundiata won. The "Lion King" was now the king of Mali.

Sundiata's army took over smaller, nearby kingdoms and made them a part of Mali. The little kingdom grew bigger and bigger. With more land, there were more people. How would Sundiata take care of them all?

First, he built a strong ***government.*** A government makes and carries out laws for the people. Sundiata wanted good and fair laws. He wanted peace in his new empire.

Next, Sundiata made sure that Mali's farmers cleared plenty of land for food. People had been growing food in West Africa for thousands of years and knew how to farm.

Farming is still an important part of life in Mali today.

Mali's farmers planted food such as peanuts, rice, millet (a kind of grain), and beans.

Sundiata knew that farming made Mali strong. But he knew that trade would make Mali rich.

Mali

GROWS WITH TRADE

THE PEOPLE OF WEST AFRICA had been trading for thousands of years. Many traders came to Mali from North Africa. They traded goods such as beads, cowrie shells, kola nuts, crops, cloth, and ivory.

Mali was in the middle of ***trade routes*** used by thousands of people. A trade route is the path a trader takes to get from one place to another. Under Sundiata's rule, villages and cities grew along the trade routes and along the Niger River. Sundiata charged traders a ***tax*** for coming into Mali to trade. The tax was paid to the king in gold or other goods. In America, we pay taxes when we buy things. Mali grew rich on these trade taxes.

Even today, trading for slabs of salt is part of life in Mali.

Salt and Gold

The most important trade goods were gold and salt. The Empire of Mali had both salt and gold mines. Salt came from the Sahara Desert in the north, and gold was found in Mali's forests in the south. Salt was dug up from mines in big slabs. It was loaded onto camels and taken to Mali's markets. Salt was traded for gold and other goods.

People and animals in West Africa need to eat salt to live. It is so hot there that people sweat and lose the salt in their bodies. Salt was also used to keep food fresh. There were no refrigerators then, so salting the food kept it from rotting. Long ago it was harder to get salt than it is today. To these people, salt was as valuable as gold!

A New King: Mansa Musa

SUNDIATA WORKED HARD TO build the Empire of Mali, and his people loved him. In 1255 Sundiata died. What would happen to the empire he had built?

A king from Mali was called a Mansa (MAHN-suh). Mansa is a Malinke word that means king or leader. Mansa Wali, Sundiata's son, was the next king. He was a good leader and knew that trade and farming were good for Mali.

Other kings came after Mansa Wali. In 1307, a great king came. His name was Mansa Musa (MOO-suh). We know a lot about Mansa Musa because he did so much to help Mali. He helped the Empire of Mali grow stronger and richer.

This is the earliest map of Mali. It shows Mansa Musa holding a large piece of gold.

Mansa Musa loved learning about new ideas and places. He was one of the first kings of Mali to visit far-away places.

He helped people in other places learn about Mali, its riches, and its people.

Mali and Islam

Like the sons of Sundiata, Mansa Musa was a Muslim. A Muslim is a follower of Islam. Islam is a religion that began in Arabia a long time ago. The Arabic word for God is Allah [ah-LAH]. Most people in Mali today are Muslims. There are about four million Muslims in America.

Mali: THE GOLDEN AGE

MANSA MUSA TOOK CHARGE of the salt and gold trade. Mali was already rich, but he made Mali richer. He took more land and gold mines from other kingdoms. Mali doubled in size. More and more traders came to Mali with gold and other goods.

The cities along the Niger River grew. One was Timbuktu (Tim-buk-TOO). It had big trading markets, schools, and libraries. Timbuktu was one of the richest cities in the world.

WORKING HARD

The people of Mali worked hard. Each person ***specialized,*** which means they did one job well. People worked at jobs such as farming, weaving, pottery, blacksmithing, or fishing.

A huge mosque in Djenné rises over a bustling market. People still come to markets in Mali to trade goods and obtain things they need for their families.

Trading one product for another to live better is called ***interdependence.*** That means people depended or counted on getting what they needed by trading something they had.

People traded their special goods to get what they wanted. For example, a weaver traded blankets with a pottery maker to get dishes. A pottery maker traded pots with a farmer to get food.

Mansa Musa's
GREAT JOURNEY

MANSA MUSA TRIED TO DO what all good Muslims try to do. He went on a special trip to a place called Mecca, Saudi Arabia. Mecca was about 3,000 miles from Mali.

This trip to Mecca is called a Hajj [HAHJ]. All Muslims try to make a Hajj at least once in their life. When Mansa Musa made his Hajj, he took 60,000 people with him. His wife took 500 people to do things for her. All the others went to help the king and to see the world.

This painting shows what it might have looked like as Mansa Musa traveled across the desert on his famous Hajj.

Mansa Musa also took hundreds of camels. One hundred camels carried 300 pounds of gold each. It is said that Mansa Musa rode across the desert like the richest king in the world. He wore long, silk robes with colorful scarves that waved in the wind. Music was played as he rode across the desert on his fine camel.

Mansa Musa gave away gold as he rode to Mecca. Everyone talked about how rich Mali must be. After this trip, a mapmaker put Mali on a map of the world. The map showed Mansa Musa holding a piece of gold.

The Great TRADERS

MUSLIMS AND OTHER TRADERS came to Mali by desert and by river. Mansa Musa opened a new trade route to the east of Mali. Many new people came to Mali along this trade route. They came to share new ideas and to trade.

Traders from North Africa came to Mali across the Sahara Desert in camel ***caravans*** [CARE-ah-vanz]. Camel caravans were groups of people who traveled with their camels.

Camels can carry up to 350 pounds of riders and goods. They can walk many miles and go two or three days without food or water.

MANSA MUSA'S IDEAS

Mansa Musa came back from Mecca with new ideas. He saw new ideas for art, building, and learning. Mali already had art and good schools, but he wanted more. He brought Muslim people back with him to live and work in Mali.

Muslim students from far away came to Timbuktu to study. Timbuktu became a place to trade and to learn. Mansa Musa thought learning was very important.

AN IMPORTANT ANIMAL

Camels have fleshy pads on their feet. These pads keep them from sinking in sand. On the tips of their pads are two toes that each have a tiny toenail or hoof. Their feet stay on top of the sand like snowshoes in snow. Camels are called the ships of the desert.

The Empire COMES TO AN END

MANSA MUSA WAS ONE of Mali's greatest kings. He helped Mali grow very rich with the salt and gold trade. He filled Mali's cities with schools, busy markets, and beautiful ***mosques*** (MOSKS). Mosques are places where Muslims gather to pray.

Mansa Musa died in 1337, and things in Mali soon changed. The kings after Mansa Musa did not keep Mali safe. Other kingdoms wanted to take over Mali, and they fought for Mali's land. The fighting weakened Mali and its army got smaller.

This building in Timbuktu is a mosque, the worship place used in Islam. It was built more than 600 years ago, during the days of Mali's empire.

In one attack by outsiders, Timbuktu was set on fire, and the schools and markets were burned.

After years of fighting, the empire of Mali came to an end. The next great kingdom in West Africa was called Songhay.

This map shows the three ancient kingdoms of West Africa.

LIFE TODAY

MALI TODAY IS DIFFERENT from Mali long ago. Mali is no longer a rich empire. Many of the people are poor and work hard to make a living. The land is dry and sometimes there is not enough water.

Still, the people of Mali are proud. Family is important, and they love art, music, and colorful clothing. Traders still use the Niger River to travel from market to market selling goods. The markets are still busy with many people.

Trading on the Niger River is still a part of life in Mali today.

Griots are storytellers in Mali. Griots can be men or women.

Mali has come a long way from the days of Sundiata and Mansa Musa. Camels still come to Mali, but not like in the past. Cars and trucks now carry people from city to city.

The people of Mali today remember their proud past. The songs and stories will be told again and again to the children of Mali, who hold the future in their hands.

Keeping the Past Alive

Today the people of Mali remember their past with stories of great kings and riches of ancient Mali. The stories of Mali's golden past are still told by ***griots.*** Griots do more than tell stories. The griots use songs, poetry, drama, and music. They teach the history of their people and their land, often learning it all by heart. They are sometimes called "the keepers of history" or the "keepers of memories."

The people of West Africa continue to listen to and learn from the griots. It is said that "when a griot dies, a library burns down." What do you think that means?

Glossary

archaeologists	Scientists who study objects from the past.
caravans	Groups of people who travel on camels.
clans	Groups of people who are part of the same large family.
government	People and organizations that make and keep laws for the people of a nation.
griots	West African storytellers
Hajj	A Muslim's trip to Mecca.
herders	People who keep sheep, cows, and other animals that live in herds, which means groups.
interdependence	When people each do different sorts of work, then trade their work and skills with one another for things they need.
kingdom	A type of nation ruled by a king or other royal person.
mosques	Holy places where Muslims gather to pray.
specialized	Doing one thing very well, instead of doing many things.
trade routes	Paths taken over and over by traders to get from place to place.
tax	Money paid in addition to the price paid for for goods. Taxes are paid to governments to help run cities and countries.

Find Out More About Mali

Mansa Musa, BY KHEPHRA BURNS (GULLIVER BOOKS, 2000)

This wonderful picture book tells the story of young Mansa Musa and his path to greatness. It includes a wonderful tale of his important journey to Mecca.

West African Kingdoms BY JULIE NELSON (RAINTREE-STECK VAUGHAN, 2001)

In this book, learn more details about the kingdoms that came before and after Mali.

Sundiata: Lion King of Mali, BY DAVID WISNIEWSKI (CLARION BOOKS, 1999)

Based on legends and fact, this book tells the story of Sundiata's time as Mali's leader.

Mali: Land of Gold and Glory, BY JOY MASOFF (FIVE PONDS PRESS, 2002)

The importance of trade plays a big part in this story of the Empire of Mali.

Faces: The Magazine About People, VOLUME 13, NO. 6, FEB. 1998

This issue covers life in Mali today.

index

credits

PHOTOGRAPHS/ILLUSTRATIONS

Khephra Burns, reprinted with permission of Harcourt Inc.: 23. David Conrad: 5, 10, 29. Corbis: 7, 15, 17, 26. Christine Drake: 21, 24, 28. Courtesy Museum of African Art, photos by Jerry L. Thompson: 9 and cover (Pace Primitive Gallery), 11 (collection of Barbara and Wayne Amedee). Societe Bibliotecque: cover and 19. Virginia Museum of Fine Arts, Richdmon/Katherine Wetzel: 8 (The Adolph D. and Wilkins C. Williams Fund). Map on page 27 painted by Itoko Maeno. Border illustration by Matti Berglund. Map on page 4 created by John Hoar; ©Virginia Museum of Fine Arts.

Author

Melanie Zucker Stanley works as a Social Studies Specialist for Fairfax County, Virginia, developing materials for teachers and children. She also works as a freelance writer, storyteller, and photographer. Her passion is history, and she enjoys bringing history to life for children. She lives with her husband, Tim, and two children, Aaron and Melanie, in Herndon, Virginia.